Lactose-Free Smoothies

Everyday blender recipes for dairy-free beverages

Conclusion 36

Disclaimer

Introduction

In past few decades, the term lactose intolerant has been used very frequently and it makes many of us wonder what in the world it really is? Lactose intolerance is a gastro-intestinal or in other words, a digestive track condition that is the result of a deficiency or weak functioning of enzyme Lactase. This digestive track enzyme is responsible for breaking down and digesting the milk sugar known as disaccharide lactose. The lactase enzyme starts up a chemical reaction which breaks this milk sugar down into glucose and galactose. A person with lactose intolerance either does not produce enzyme lactase or does not produce enough. This lactase deficiency results in inability to digest milk or milk derivatives that are part of our daily diet. Common symptoms of lactose intolerance consist of abdominal bloating, gas, cramps, diarrhea or even nausea and vomiting after consuming dairy products. Studies have shown that people suffering from lactase deficiency tend to also suffer from inflammatory bowel disease after milk consumption.

Advances in genetics and recent research have shown that lactose intolerance is rather a genetically-determined characteristic then a disorder. A genetic mutation that is usually present at birth, leads to this less production of enzyme lactase in the body resulting in abdominal discomfort and other severe symptoms. However, there is something known as a secondary lactose intolerance which is a result of a destruction of intestinal lining due to some other primary diseases or factors.

Currently, lactose intolerance can be managed by making some behavioral changes such as modifying daily diet. It can also be managed by taking lactase enzyme supplements. However, complete abandonment of dairy products is not advised as it can lead to serious deficiencies of other vitamins and minerals such as Vitamin D and calcium etc. If a person is to choose a complete dairy free diet profile, they should discuss their supplement intake options with their doctor so they do not become deficient on calcium and other vitamins dairy has to offer.

Though reduction in the consumption of dairy products seems like an easier and least expansive alternative, the loss of nutrition as a result is a very strong factor to consider before making such decisions. Luckily many alternatives to milk and other milk-derivatives are available to us today, which means that we can make up a good chunk of lost nutrition by using these alternatives. People who experience lactose intolerance can tap into a whole range of healthy and nutritious alternatives without having to punish their taste buds.

This book was written for precisely that reason. I wanted to provide a range of alternatives for nutritious and delicious beverages that will have your taste buds scream for more. This book provides you with a variety of smoothie recipes that do not use milk or any milk-derivatives. This book is divided in four sections, each section providing a range of recipes pertaining to a particular kind of milk alternative. It offers you a list of smoothies that are made using alternatives such as Coconut, Soy, Almond, and rice milk.   Let us look at the benefits of these dairy alternatives used as a base for lactose-free smoothies.

Coconut milk

Coconut milk is produced from the grated meat of a coconut. A point to be noted here is that coconut milk is not the same as coconut water. While coconut water is the liquid that is found in the hollow middle part of the fruit, coconut milk is made from grated meat of the coconut. Though it has a slightly higher content of saturated fats but it is chock full of omega 3, 6, and 9 fats and other amino acids that are very beneficial to human body. It is very famous as a food ingredient in Southeast Asia.

Coconut milk can be very beneficial for people suffering from secondary lactose intolerance. As stated previously, some diseases such as Crohn's disease, irritable bowel syndrome, gastritis, and certain intestinal cancers can destroy the intestinal lining. Coconut milk has ingredients that have shown healing of intestinal lining in many patients. In addition, coconut milk has a high fiber content which keeps you full longer. It is also a good source of iron, calcium, and potassium.

Almond milk

Almond milk is often used as a substitute for dairy milk and it is made from ground almonds. It is slightly beige in color and has a nutty taste with a fairly creamy texture. Many people can easily make almond milk at home. However for all others like us, it can also be purchased in long-life cartons which are easily available in many grocery stores all over the U.S. Almond milk is a very healthy, nutritious, and delicious alternative to dairy and certainly ranks higher than rice milk on all three of these aspects unless it can't be used due to allergy reasons.

It is naturally cholesterol free and does not contain any lactose like the animal milk. Since it does not contain any animal products, it is suitable for all vegetarians or vegan diets. Almonds are high on calcium and low on sugar which makes them a better alternative for people with diabetes. Almonds also have high a quantity of vitamin E which benefits both eyes and the skin.

Soy milk

Soy milk also known as Soya milk is made from soybeans. It is a stable emulsion of oil, water and protein. It is produced by soaking dry soybeans and then grinding them with water. It contains same proportion of proteins, carbohydrates and ash as cow's milk but is free of lactose. It can also be produced at home with the traditional kitchen tools or with soy milk machine.

In addition to being a good dairy alternative, soy milk is also heart healthy. Regular dairy products are high on saturated fats and cholesterol but soy milk has zero cholesterol and has mainly unsaturated fats. According to research studies, Soy milk helps in reduction of bad cholesterol as it has a high content of omega-3 and omega-6 fatty acids.

Soy milk can also prevent men against prostate cancer as it contains a plant based hormone known as phyto-estrogen known to reduce the secretion of testosterone in human body. For the same reason just described, soy milk also helps postmenopausal women who have reduced natural production of estrogen. Postmenopausal women have a much higher risk of high blood pressure and heart disease due to this shortage of estrogen in their body and they can reduce such risks by consuming soy milk on a regular basis.

Rice milk

As the name suggests, rice milk is grain based milk which is derived from processed white or brown rice. It can be found unsweetened and it can be sweetened using sugarcane syrup or other sugars. Now days, rice milk is easily available in most local grocery stores in the U.S. It is also offered in a variety of flavors such as vanilla and chocolate.

The greatest benefit of rice milk is that it has the lowest allergy risk associated with it, out of all other milk alternative products and it is lactose free. Once again, rice milk is also free of saturated fats and cholesterol making it part of a heart healthy diet. Rice milk is high on minerals and B vitamins which are essential for boosting metabolism and cancer prevention.

While keeping all the benefits of rice milk in mind, a word of caution is in order. As many benefits as the rice milk offers, people with diabetes should be cautious about using rice milk or making it a regular part of their diet as it contains a high amount of carbohydrates, which is not suitable for a person with diabetes.

All the alternatives mentioned previously have their own strengths and weaknesses. What you choose to make a part of your diet, would be your choice. However, if conditions beyond your control such as lactose intolerance force you to keep certain ingredients off from your table, it should not mean that you don't have other options at your disposal. The pain and discomfort associated with lactose intolerance can be avoided with certain modifications to your dietary behavior while still keeping your diet rich in nutrition. Who says that the behavioral modification and dietary changes can only be accomplished by sacrificing taste? This book will show you that you can enjoy a variety of delicious and nutritious smoothies without the inclusion of any dairy products, the only special equipment you need is a blender. So enjoy these lactose-free smoothies that are so yummy and are easy on your tummy!

Coconut Milk Smoothies

Strawberry & Banana Smoothie

This delightful and refreshing smoothie is not only mouthwatering but also filled with the flavors of extremely healthy fruits like strawberry and banana. Strawberry is rich in vitamins and also protects teeth and heart. Like strawberry, banana is also rich in vitamins which help you in improving eye health, hypertension and fight against cancer.

Servings: 4

Ingredients:

4 cups unsweetened coconut milk

2 frozen bananas, peeled and sliced

2½ cups fresh strawberries, hulled and sliced

Directions:

1. In a blender, add all ingredients and blend till smooth and frothy.
2. Ice can also be added to the blender if you prefer icy smoothies. Otherwise, you can add some ice-cubes to chill the smoothie and serve.

Spinach, Papaya& Pineapple Smoothie

This smoothie is so refreshing and full of minerals and vitamins. Spinach helps us in many ways as it improves vision, skin and bone health. Whereas, pineapple strengthens bones and gums too. It also fights against cold and sore throat. Papaya is great for skin health and has anti-nausea properties. If you are not a vegetable lover, this is a great recipe to disguise vegetables among such sweet tropical fruits and feel good about making a healthy choice.

Servings: 4

Ingredients:

4 cups unsweetened coconut milk

6 cups baby spinach, trimmed

2 cups papayas, peeled, seeded and sliced

3 cups pineapple chunks with juice

Directions:

1. In a blender, add all ingredients and blend till smooth and frothy.
2. Ice can also be added to the blender if you prefer icy smoothies. Otherwise, you can add some ice-cubes to chill the smoothie and serve.

Spiced Peach Smoothie

Peach and spices make a delicious and perfect combo in this smoothie. Peach is a rich source of antioxidant, vitamins and fiber. It helps in controlling cancer and heart disease. In addition to the healthy benefits of peaches, spices give a nice flavorful kick to this smoothie. This smoothie is practically a dessert in the liquid form and it is a healthy alternative to satisfy your sweet tooth.

Servings: 4

Ingredients:

4 cups unsweetened coconut milk

6 peaches, peeled, pitted, sliced and frozen

2 teaspoons honey

1 cup oats

2 teaspoons vanilla extract

Pinch of nutmeg powder

¼ teaspoon cinnamon powder

Pinch of salt

Directions:

1. In a blender, add all ingredients and blend till smooth and frothy.

2. Ice can also be added to the blender if you prefer icy smoothies. Otherwise, you can add some ice-cubes to chill the smoothie and serve.

Berry Blast Smoothie

This berry blast smoothie is delicious and loaded with essential nutrients to help you start your day off right. This smoothie is rich in vitamins and chock full of antioxidants to help support your immune system and to keep you energized throughout your day.

Servings: 4

Ingredients:

4 cups unsweetened coconut milk

4 cups frozen strawberries

4 cups frozen blueberries

2cups frozen raspberries

2tablespoons agave nectar

Directions:

1. In a blender, add all ingredients and blend till smooth and frothy.
2. Ice can also be added to the blender if you prefer icy smoothies. Otherwise, you can add some ice-cubes to chill the smoothie and serve.

Spinach, Honey Dew & Banana Smoothie

The ingredients of this refreshing smoothie are simple and affordable. Banana provides a rich and creamy texture to this spinach smoothie. Spinach and banana are rich in vitamins. Both are beneficial for eye health. Ripe honey dew is very sweet and juicy and combined with the creaminess of bananas, it gives this recipe just the right amount of texture and sweetness.

Servings: 4

Ingredients:

4 cups unsweetened coconut milk

6 cups raw spinach, trimmed

2 cups honey dew melon chunks

1 ripe banana peeled and sliced

1tablespoon honey

Directions:

1. In a blender, add all ingredients and blend till smooth and frothy.
2. Ice can also be added to the blender if you prefer icy smoothies. Otherwise, you can add some ice-cubes to chill the smoothie and serve.

Almond Milk Smoothies

Banana, Coconut & Chocolate Chip Smoothie

This flavorful smoothie is a concoction of two healthy fruits which keep you satisfied for a long period. Banana contains the highest content of potassium out of all fruits which helps in controlling hypertension. Coconut is highly nutritious and also rich in vitamins. Like these healthy fruits oats and almonds are also packed with vitamins, protein and minerals.

Servings: 4

Ingredients:

3 cups unsweetened almond milk

4 tablespoons coconut flakes

4 ripe bananas, peeled and sliced

1½ tablespoons almond butter

1 cup oats

1 tablespoon raw almonds, crushed

3 tablespoons raw cacao nibs (organic, raw unsweetened chocolate chips)

1tablespoon honey

Directions:

1. In a blender, add all ingredients and blend till smooth and frothy.
2. Ice can also be added to the blender if you prefer icy smoothies. Otherwise, you can add some ice-cubes to chill the smoothie and serve.

Ginger, Spinach & Blueberry Smoothie

This smoothie is not only delicious but also is a great way to get nutritional benefits of an ingredient like ginger into your body. With blueberries and ginger, you are able to combine the sweet and peppery flavors together and take advantage of the nutrients offered by both. Ginger helps in curing of cold, sore throat and stomach discomfort. Both blueberry and ginger fight against cancer.

Servings: 4

Ingredients:

2½ cups unsweetened almond milk

½ cup coconut flakes or coconut milk

1½ cups frozen blueberries

3 teaspoons fresh ginger, grated

2 cups spinach, trimmed

1tablespoon honey

Directions:

1. In a blender, add all ingredients and blend till smooth and frothy.
2. Ice can also be added to the blender if you prefer icy smoothies. Otherwise, you can add some ice-cubes to chill the smoothie and serve.

Pineapple & Cantaloupe Smoothie

This refreshing, juicy and cool smoothie is a beautiful combination of pineapple and cantaloupe. It is flavorful and full of nutrients. Vitamins filled pineapple strengthens bones and gums. It also fights against cold and sore throat. Like pineapple, cantaloupe is also rich in vitamins and fiber. It also promotes the health of heart and lungs. This smoothie not only tastes good but it's beautiful color will make you feel like you are on an exotic vacation.

Servings: 4

Ingredients:

3 cups unsweetened almond milk

4 cups fresh cantaloupe

4 cups pineapple chunks

Directions:

1. In a blender, add all ingredients and blend till smooth and frothy.
2. Ice can also be added to the blender if you prefer icy smoothies. Otherwise, you can add some ice-cubes to chill the smoothie and serve.

Kale, bananas, Peach & Raspberry Smoothie

This simple but incredibly delicious smoothie is made with peach, banana and nutritious kale. Banana adds some creaminess to this smoothie. Peaches are a rich source of antioxidants, vitamins and fiber. Raspberries complement peach nicely in this recipe and add a gourmet touch to it. Like peach, kale is also rich in antioxidant and fiber. What's more, you can disguise your daily vegetable intake in this delicious drink and have a guilt-free sweet treat.

Servings: 4

Ingredients:

3 cups unsweetened almond milk

1-2 cups frozen bananas, peeled and sliced

2 cups frozen peaches, pitted and sliced

2 cups fresh or frozen raspberries

4 cups fresh kale, trimmed

2 teaspoons honey

Directions:

1. In a blender, add all ingredients and blend till smooth and frothy.
2. Ice can also be added to the blender if you prefer icy smoothies. Otherwise, you can add some ice-cubes to chill the smoothie and serve.

Banana, Walnuts & Cinnamon Smoothie

This banana smoothie gives your body an extra boost in the morning time. It is filled with the nutrients of healthy banana. Both banana and cinnamon go very well together in this classic smoothie. Maple syrup in this recipe gives an additional unique sweetness to this smoothie. Addition of warm winter spice and nuts such as cinnamon and walnuts to this recipe will make any day seem like a holiday.

Servings: 4

Ingredients:

3 cups unsweetened almond milk

4 frozen bananas, peeled and sliced

½ cup chopped walnuts

½ teaspoon vanilla extract

1¼ teaspoon cinnamon powder

1 teaspoons maple syrup

Directions:

1. In a blender, add all ingredients and blend till smooth and frothy.
2. Ice can also be added to the blender if you prefer icy smoothies. Otherwise, you can add some ice-cubes to chill the smoothie and serve.

Soy Milk Smoothies

Strawberry & Avocado Smoothie

This strawberry and avocado smoothie tastes more like a dessert rather than a drink. Avocado adds a creamy texture to this smoothie. Both strawberry and avocados are packed with the disease fighting antioxidants. Strawberry helps in fighting the heart disease. Avocados are loaded with good cholesterol and are very heart healthy. Avocados are a great addition to your diet for jump starting your weight loss regimen. Addition of healthy grain such as flax seed also makes this recipe tummy friendly.

Servings: 4

Ingredients:

3 cups soy milk

1½ cups fresh strawberries, hulled and sliced

1 large avocado, peeled, pitted and sliced

1 tablespoon honey

2 teaspoons flaxseeds

Directions:

1. In a blender, add all ingredients and blend till smooth and frothy.

2. Ice can also be added to the blender if you prefer icy smoothies. Otherwise, you can add some ice-cubes to chill the smoothie and serve.

Pineapple, Banana, & mango Smoothie

This recipe is full of tropical flavors. For the days you cannot make it to a tropical paradise, the taste of this smoothie will bring the paradise right at home.

Servings: 4

Ingredients:

3 cups soy milk

2 cups pineapple chunks with juice

2 frozen bananas, peeled and sliced

2 cups frozen diced mangos

1 teaspoon vanilla extract

Directions:

1. In a blender, add all ingredients and blend till smooth and frothy.
2. Ice can also be added to the blender if you prefer icy smoothies. Otherwise, you can add some ice-cubes to chill the smoothie and serve.

Mixed Fruit & Kale Smoothie

This is a super delicious smoothie with mixed fruits and kale. Mixed fruit turn bitter kale into a sweet, delightful and immune-boosting smoothie. All of these fruits are rich in vitamins. This recipe can be adjusted according to the availability of different fruits depending on the season. So go on and experiment, add or remove what you like or don't like and it is sure to taste wonderful.

Servings: 4

Ingredients:

3 cups soy milk

3 cups fresh kale, trimmed

2 frozen bananas, peeled and sliced

1 mango, peeled, pitted and cubed

3 oranges, peeled, seeded and sectioned

1 cup strawberries (hulled)

2 cups frozen peaches

Directions:

1. In a blender, add all ingredients and blend till smooth and frothy.
2. Ice can also be added to the blender if you prefer icy smoothies. Otherwise, you can add

some ice-cubes to chill the smoothie and serve.

Kiwi, Cucumber & Melon Smoothie

This is very refreshing and tasty smoothie. Rich in vitamin and fiber, kiwi facilitates weight loss and promotes general health also. Melon fights against many diseases such as cancer and kidney problems. This recipe gives a great opportunity to disguise vegetables among the sweetness of honey and Kiwi and meet your daily vegetable serving requirements.

Servings: 4

Ingredients:

3 cups soy milk

7 kiwis cut into quarts

4 cups melon, peeled, seeded and cubed

1/2 cucumber peeled, seeded and diced

1 tablespoon honey

Directions:

1. In a blender, add all ingredients and blend till smooth and frothy.
2. Ice can also be added to the blender if you prefer icy smoothies. Otherwise, you can add some ice-cubes to chill the smoothie and serve.

Watermelon, Banana & Blueberry Smoothie

This cool, light and refreshing smoothie is excellent on a hot summer day. Frozen bananas add creaminess to this refreshing smoothie while berries boost your immunity. Watermelon is rich in vitamin and fiber and is great for hydration on a hot summer day.

Servings: 4

Ingredients:

3 cups soy milk

7 cups watermelon, seeded and cubed

1 frozen bananas, peeled and sliced

2 cups blueberries

Pinch of salt (optional)

Directions:

1. In a blender, add all ingredients and blend till smooth and frothy.
2. Ice can also be added to the blender if you prefer icy smoothies. Otherwise, you can add some ice-cubes to chill the smoothie and serve.

Rice Milk Smoothies

Mango, Banana & Raspberry Smoothie

This tasty and healthy smoothie goes well when temperature climbs high. Mango is rich in vitamins, fiber and potassium. It improves eye health and immune system. It also fights against cancer and high cholesterol. A combination of mango, raspberries, and banana makes this recipe a good alternative to other tropical smoothie recipes.

Servings: 4

Ingredients:

3 cups rice milk

1 frozen bananas, peeled and sliced

2 frozen mangoes, pitted and sliced

3 cups frozen raspberries

Directions:

1. In a blender, add all ingredients and blend till smooth and frothy.
2. Ice can also be added to the blender if you prefer icy smoothies. Otherwise, you can add some ice-cubes to chill the smoothie and serve.

Peanut Butter & Banana Smoothie

If you are a peanut butter lover, this recipe is an awesome treat to satisfy your sweet tooth while providing you with ton of protein from the peanut butter to keep you full longer. This smoothie is a peanut butter and banana sandwich in a cup but only better since it doesn't contain added calories of bread. So if you feel up to having a guilt-free dessert, you are on the right page of this recipe book.

Servings: 4

Ingredients:

3 cups rice milk

1 cup peanut butter (preferably creamy)

2 frozen bananas, peeled and sliced

2 teaspoons honey

Directions:

1. In a blender, add all ingredients and blend till smooth and frothy.
2. Ice can also be added to the blender if you prefer icy smoothies. Otherwise, you can add some ice-cubes to chill the smoothie and serve.

Apples, Peach, & Spinach Smoothie

Spinach is considered one of the healthiest foods due to its high iron content and antioxidants. It improves vision, skin and bone health. Bananas and apple together create a sweet and sour taste that makes spinach more palatable. Peaches along with cinnamon powder give this smoothie the aroma of a dessert.

Servings: 4

Ingredients:

3 cups rice milk

2-3 apples peeled and sliced (any apples of your choice, use Granny Smiths for some tartness)

6 cups fresh spinach, trimmed

1 tablespoon honey

2 cups frozen peaches

Pinch of cinnamon powder

Directions:

1. In a blender, add all ingredients and blend till smooth and frothy.
2. Ice can also be added to the blender if you prefer icy smoothies. Otherwise, you can add some ice-cubes to chill the smoothie and serve.

Tropical Fruit Smoothie with Dates & Macadamia Nuts

The tropical fruits give this refreshing smoothie a crowning touch. It will be a great and healthy snack for your toddlers too. These tropical fruits provide many goodies to your body's wellness just like eyes health, weight loss and healing of wounds. Dates are a very beneficial fruit from the middle-eastern region and add a unique sweetness to this beverage.

Servings: 4

Ingredients:

3 cups rice milk

2 frozen bananas, peeled and sliced

1 large papaya, peeled, seeded and cubed

1 large mango, peeled, pitted and cubed

10 dates, pitted and sliced

¼ cup macadamia nuts, toasted

Directions:

1. In a blender, add all ingredients and blend till smooth and frothy.
2. Ice can also be added to the blender if you prefer icy smoothies. Otherwise, you can add some ice-cubes to chill the smoothie and serve.

Chocolaty Strawberry & Raspberry Smoothie

This smoothie is perfect for a healthy start of the day. This strawberry smoothie gets an extra touch of flavor from cocoa. For those days when you just cannot do without chocolate but you still don't want to be unhealthy, this would be the perfect recipe to try. Satisfy your chocolate cravings without feeling guilty.

Servings: 4

Ingredients:

3 cups rice milk

2 cups frozen strawberries

2 cups fresh or frozen raspberries

2 bananas peeled and sliced

4 tablespoons cocoa powder

2 teaspoons vanilla extract

2 tablespoon honey

Directions:

1. In a blender, add all ingredients and blend till smooth and frothy.
2. Ice can also be added to the blender if you prefer icy smoothies. Otherwise, you can add some ice-cubes to chill the smoothie and serve.

Conclusion

As you can see the recipes included in this book offer a variety of smoothie recipes that utilize four different non-dairy alternatives as a base ingredient. Becoming dairy-free is not impossible and it also does not have to take away the variety of ingredients from your menu. All of the recipes are easily made in a blender and can be easily adjusted by adding or removing the ingredients you prefer or do not prefer to use. These recipes are nutritious, delicious and full of proteins and carbohydrates. You can get the best of both worlds; great health and exotic fruit flavors. These smoothies can easily be on your everyday meal plan while keeping you away from the tummy troubles lactose-intolerance brings with it.

So, stock up your pantry & refrigerator with these nutritious and delicious dairy alternatives and give your blender a good work out. Needing a special diet does not and should not limit your options. So consider your tummy troubles a thing of the past, with these recipes in your hands you will not miss milk or other dairy derivatives. Use this book as a basic recipe guide and you will be a lactose-free smoothie expert in no time.

Made in the USA
Las Vegas, NV
21 December 2022

63807838R00022